Life on Other Planets

Rhonda Lucas Donald

Franklin Watts
A Division of Scholastic Inc.
New York • Toronto • London • Auckland • Sydney
Mexico City • New Delhi • Hong Kong
Danbury, Connecticut

Note to readers: Definitions for words in **bold** can be found in the Glossary at the back of this book.

I would like to thank the following scientists for reviewing this book and making many helpful suggestions: William Boynton, professor of cosmochemistry and geochemistry in the Department of Planetary Sciences at the University of Arizona; Debra Fischer, postdoctoral fellow at the University of California, Berkeley; Stephen Giovannoni, professor of microbiology at Oregon State University; Mary Hardin and Guy Webster at NASA's Jet Propulsion Lab; David Morrison, chief scientist for the NASA Astrobiology Institute; Seth Shostack, astronomer with SETI; Kathie Thomas-Keprta, astrobiologist at NASA's Johnson Space Center.

Photographs © 2003: Corbis Images: 48 (Bettmann), 10 (Dennis di Cicco), 7 (Charles O'Rear), 18 (Ralph White), 6; Corbis Sygma/NASA/SUSAN: 3 left, 39; NASA: 9 (Jeff Hester and Paul Scowen/Arizona State University), cover (Mohammad Heydari-Malayeri, Paris Observatory France/ESA), 40 (J. McClintock), 24 (The Hubble Heritage Team), 36; Peter Arnold Inc.: 4 (Binnewies/Sporenberg/Astrofoto), 29 (Michael Carroll/Astrofoto), 11 (Manfred Kage), 26 right, 27, 31 (NASA), 26 left, 30, 34 (NASA/Astrofoto), 32 (NASA/JPL/CALTECH/ Astrofoto), 12 (NOAA GOES/NASA/Astrofoto), 3 right, 46 (Van Ravenswaay/Astrofoto), 14 (Kevin Schafer), 45 (Richard J. Wainscoat), 17 (Bruno P. Zehnder); Photo Researchers, NY: 28 (Julian Baum/SPL), 22 (Wolfgang Baumeister), 52 (Dr. Seth Shostak/SPL), 21 (Kaj R. Svensson/SPL); Robertstock.com: 19 (J. Blank), 33, 38; The Image Works/Photri/Topham: 42.

Library of Congress Cataloging-in-Publication Data

Donald, Rhonda Lucas, 1962-
    Life on other planets / by Rhonda Lucas Donald.
        p. cm. — (Watts Library)
    Summary: A comprehensive look at the question of whether there is life on other planets, from the imaginative visions of fantasy novels and science fiction movies to the facts revealed by today's cutting-edge technology.
    Includes bibliographical references and index.
    ISBN 0-531-12280-8 (lib. bdg.)   0-531-16374-1 (pbk.)
    1. Life on other planets—Juvenile literature. [1. Life on other planets.] I. Title. II. Series.
QB54.D66 2003
576.8'39—dc21
                                                                    2003005817

Contents

Radio telescopes, such as this one in Chile, photographed during a meteor shower, are used to record and analyze sound from the farthest reaches of space.

Chapter One

Is Anybody Out There?

Are humans and other living things on Earth alone in the universe? That is one of science's biggest questions. So far, we've found no proof of living things anywhere else. But our search for life outside of Earth—**extraterrestrial** life— is really just beginning. Life's ingredients are scattered throughout the universe. And we've found living things thriving in what seem like impossible environments on Earth. Maybe life could exist in the extreme conditions of other planets or moons. If so, where would it most likely be? How might we track it down? And what would alien life be like? These are some of the questions this book will try to answer. But first, let's take a look at the nature of life on Earth and how it might have begun.

A Recipe for Life

For life on Earth to exist, you need at least three things:

1. organic molecules
2. water
3. energy

All organic, or living, cells on Earth contain carbon. Carbon is an **element**, a substance that contains only one type of atom. Carbon is a good life-forming element because it combines with other elements to make other things. On Earth, water is the stuff that allows tiny bits of carbon-based material called **organic molecules** to move around, dissolve, and combine. About two-thirds of the human body is water. Even microscopic living things called **microbes** that survive miles

Diamonds are a form of carbon, the element found in all known life. So, we really all are diamonds in the rough!

Life of Another Type

Silicon, an element found in sand, might also be the basis for life-forming molecules in an extraterrestrial environment. The shaggy, rock-tunneling horta from the original *Star Trek* television series was supposed to be a silicon-based creature.

deep in ice or beneath solid rock need at least some liquid water. Most life on Earth lives in the ocean. So from what we know, life needs some sort of liquid that allows the organic molecules to move around, bump into each other, and combine. On a world without water, liquid forms of ammonia or methane might serve the same purpose.

Even if we limit our search for extraterrestrial life to carbon-based molecules and water, there are plenty of places to look. Organic molecules and water in the form of ice are found throughout the universe. They exist in **meteorites**, or chunks of space rock that have landed on Earth; on planets and moons in our solar system; and in **interstellar** clouds—the gas and dust among the stars. Why are organic molecules and ice so common? They are some of what's left after a star forms. For life to have a chance, the ice needs to melt and a third ingredient must be present—energy.

The Sun provides the energy that drives most life on Earth. Plants use the Sun's energy to make food in a process called **photosynthesis**. Without the plants on land and in the upper ocean, most animals could not exist. Animals eat plants, and other animals eat the plant-eating animals. On Earth, plants are the basis of the food chain.

In recent years, scientists have found living things that don't need sunlight to survive. Sunlight cannot reach the deep ocean floor, so there are no plants there. But microbes get what they need to live from the heat and chemicals that pour through cracks in Earth's crust. The heat comes from a layer beneath Earth's surface that is made of partly molten rock. So in our search for life, we might look in places that have either stars like our Sun or underground heat.

How Did Life Begin?

So you've got the three ingredients for life: organic molecules, water, and energy. Since these things exist together in many places in the universe, why haven't we found lots of other life-forms? Hey, we're still looking! But life doesn't automatically erupt when these ingredients are present. No one yet understands how life began on Earth. That's another of science's big questions. Scientists do have some ideas, though.

Everything began with a bang—the **Big Bang**. That's the name for the explosion that gave birth to the universe about 15 billion years ago. The first stars formed after the Big Bang. Some of the stars exploded to form clouds called **nebulas**, which contain organic molecules, water, and other compounds. Eventually nebulas formed more stars. Some of these stars anchor their own solar systems, with planets, **comets**, and **asteroids** surrounding them.

In the Eagle nebula you can see gas and dust combining to form new stars.

Comet Hale-Bopp makes its way across space. Scientists believe that comets and meteorites may have long ago brought water, in the form of ice, from the outer reaches of space to Earth.

In our solar system, Earth was in just the right place for life to begin. It was close enough to the Sun for liquid water to exist. Before there was life on Earth, there was an ocean, still lifeless. There were also volcanoes spewing ash and chemicals into the **atmosphere**. Comets and meteorites carrying ice and organic molecules may have brought some of the building blocks of life crashing to Earth. About 4 billion years ago, all the ingredients were mixed up in Earth's soup pot. Scientists think life on Earth resulted from a combination of the right ingredients and chemical processes.

The first "Earthlings" were single-celled **microorganisms**. Over vast amounts of time, the single-celled organisms evolved into multicelled marine life such as jellyfish. Primitive

Shown here are plankton—microscopic organisms that float in the ocean or other waters. As the basis of Earth's food chain and the major supplier of oxygen on the planet, they are essential to life.

Is Earth Rare?

Many scientists believe that life could be common in the universe. But geologist Peter Ward and astronomer Donald Brownlee say that the formation of life on Earth was unique. Their idea is called the Rare Earth hypothesis. They point out that Earth **orbit**s, or circles, the Sun in a habitable, or livable, zone. And gas giant Jupiter sucks up many of the asteroids and comets that might strike Earth, wiping out living things. Ward and Brownlee think the odds of another planet having such favorable conditions for advanced life such as that on Earth are low.

plant life also developed. It has only been in the past 550 million years that more advanced life emerged. First came shellfish, and then fish, amphibians, reptiles, and mammals.

A Is for Astrobiology

Astrobiology is the study of extraterrestrial life. Astrobiologists may specialize in areas such as astronomy, biology, chemistry, geology, or physics. They combine their knowledge to explore how life began on Earth and how and where it might form elsewhere in the universe. They have a tough job. The only life we know of is on Earth, so these scientists learn as much as they can about life here. They then apply that knowledge to speculate about how life might exist somewhere else. Of course they are also searching for signs of life elsewhere. The remaining chapters of this book describe some of the places and ways they are looking.

Smoke rises from thermal vents in Leihrnjukur, Iceland. Scientists have recently discovered that such vents can be home to unusual forms of life.

Chapter Two

Extreme Living

The dry surface of Mars or the frozen seas of Jupiter's moon Europa may seem like inhospitable places for life. But we've got some pretty unfriendly places to live right here on Earth, yet some amazing organisms call them home. Studying **extremophiles**—living things that thrive in extreme surroundings—may help us understand how life might exist on another world. How extreme is an extremophile's environment? Think cold—freezing cold. Or boiling hot. Or poisonous. Or made of solid rock. Now you're getting the idea.

Icy Inhabitants

The McMurdo Dry Valleys of Antarctica are deserts—very cold deserts. The area gets only 2 inches (6 centimeters) of precipitation a year, and the temperature averages 4 degrees below zero (-20° Celsius). The valleys contain lakes covered by as much as 20 feet (6 meters) of ice year-round. Scientists looking for life in the lakes instead found something living in the ice that covers them.

The team was drilling into solid ice. About 6 feet (2 m) down the ice, they hit a layer of gravel. A closer look showed small amounts of liquid water. How could there be liquid water amid all that ice? It seems that the water forms during the Antarctic summer, when there is a brief thaw. Where there's water, there might be life. Sure enough, the scientists found microorganisms living there—blue green algae and bacteria that look like beaded necklaces. The microbes get everything they need to live and grow during the thaw, even though the temperature never reaches more than a degree or so above freezing. When the ice freezes again, the organisms go dormant, or inactive, until the next thaw. Then they "wake up" and get on with life again.

If life can exist in the middle of solid ice in Antarctica, then perhaps it can also survive in the dry, cold environment on Mars or within Europa's ice sheets. Many scientists believe it's

Opposite: Ice breaks up in McMurdo Sound, off the coast of Antarctica. Antarctica is home to living things that thrive in extreme environments, in this case, extreme cold.

possible. The *Odyssey* orbiter discovered strong evidence of ice on the surface of Mars in 2002. Hopes are high that we may find life there.

Heat Seekers

Deep on the ocean floor are cracks in Earth's crust called **hydrothermal vents**. The molten layer beneath the surface spews hot gases and minerals into the surrounding water. It is a **toxic** brew. Water spewing from such vents can reach

Thermal vents on the ocean's floor, such as this one at the bottom of the Guaymas Basin in the Gulf of California, are home to some very unusual life forms.

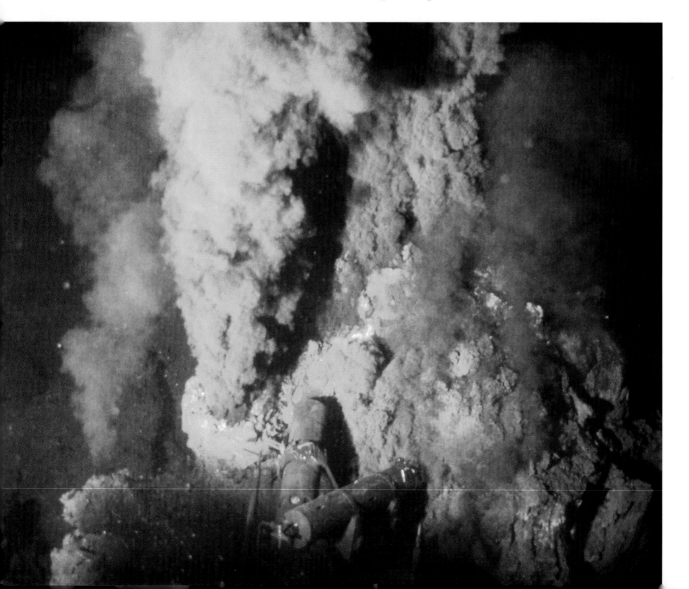

temperatures higher than 750° F (400° C). Thermal vents are places of scorching heat, poisonous chemicals, total darkness, and crushing water pressure. But they're home to a thriving community of life adapted to these seemingly impossible conditions.

Pompeii worms are the stars of these hot spots. The worms, which look like feathers, live in tubes encrusted on "chimneys" that form over the vents. The Pompeiis are among the most heat tolerant creatures on Earth, surviving in near boiling water.

Back on land, the hot springs and geysers of Yellowstone National Park bubble with microscopic plants and animals that live in the toxic water and scalding temperatures. In

This is Castle geyser in Yellowstone National Park. Inside the geysers live tiny organisms that don't mind the heat.

Iceland bacteria live in bubbling hot acid pools that form when underground steam escapes through cracks in Earth's crust. Not only do these bacteria not mind the heat, but they thrive in the acid water.

Finding heat- and chemical-tolerant life raises hopes of locating such hardy species elsewhere. What if hydrothermal vents exist on Europa or another icy world? The heat the vents produce may mean that there's a liquid ocean beneath the ice. Movement of Europa's surface ice leads scientists to believe that there may be liquid water underneath. Any planet with underground heat or volcanoes could be home to heat-loving microbes or even more advanced species such as Pompeii worms.

Rock Stars

A mile beneath the ocean floor is a community that really rocks. Scientists found it by taking core samples of the ocean floor. They gathered these samples by drilling far down into Earth's crust and bringing up sections of the rock and sediment in narrow tubes. When the team looked at layers of a

Basalt, such as that contained in these columns in British Columbia, Canada, is the most abundant of Earth's volcanic, or igneous, rocks. Basalt also covers much of the surface of the Moon.

rock called basalt, they found squiggles and trails left behind by tunneling bacteria. The bacteria actually seem to ingest the rock. Groundwater that seeps in from above meets their water needs. And the bacteria aren't alone. Tiny one-celled predators feed on the rock-loving bacteria in this underworld. Dr. Martin Fisk of Oregon State University says that in similar conditions, "Microbes could live beneath any rocky planet. It would be no problem to have life inside of Mars, or within a moon of Jupiter, or even on a comet containing ice crystals that gets warmed up when the comet passes by the Sun."

What scientists are learning about extremophiles is shaping plans for the search for life elsewhere. They now know that though life may not be found on the planet surface, it could exist deep beneath its crust or encased in ice or near a hydrothermal vent or in a mix of chemicals that would doom many living things on Earth. To an extremophile, such places would be home sweet home.

Opposite: This is a heat-loving enzyme from an extremophile bacteria. The discovery of extremophiles on Earth seems to suggest a somewhat greater possibility of life existing elsewhere in the universe.

Verne's Journey

In *A Journey to the Center of the Earth*, novelist Jules Verne wrote about explorers who descend to Earth's center through a dead volcano. They find a world populated with amazing creatures.

Verne's 1864 story is fanciful. But we have found life at surprising depths in Earth's crust. And some scientists think there might be as much life underground as on Earth's surface.

The universe is in a constant process of creation and change. This image taken by the Hubble Space Telescope *shows clusters of new stars being formed from interstellar gas and dust in galaxy NGC 4214.*

Chapter Three

Looking for "Neighbors"

Humans can't yet hop on a starship and warp off into the galaxy to greet aliens on their own turf. So we're searching for life a little closer to home—in our own solar system. Instead of starships, we're using unmanned probes and satellites to look for life. The lead agency for space exploration in the United States is **NASA, the National Aeronautics and Space Administration**.

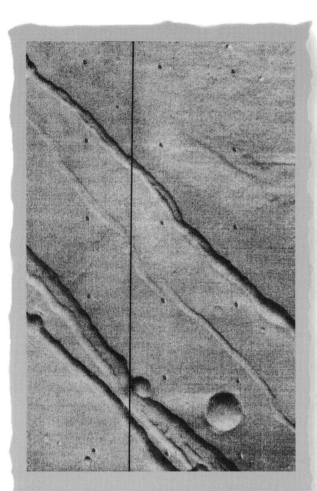

Mars Mimics

Scientists have been able to grow microorganisms in conditions similar to those on Mars. They have built a special chamber with a Mars-like environment, complete with ashen soil, a carbon dioxide atmosphere, low pressure, and cold temperatures. The organisms that have emerged in this environment have produced the gas methane (a waste product), proving that they are living.

Mars Missions

NASA's *Mariner 4* flew past Mars in 1965 and snapped the first close-up photographs of another planet. It makes sense that Mars would be the first place to search for extraterrestrial life because it is the most Earth-like planet in our solar system. *Vikings I* and *II* were the first missions to land spacecraft on

another planet. They touched down on Mars in 1976 and sent back important data until 1982. In 1997, *Mars Pathfinder*'s robotic rover clambered over Mars's rocky landscape, taking photographs. A separate lander conducted weather tests.

Mars Global Surveyor is now in orbit around the red planet. It entered orbit in 1997 and mapped the entire planet over the course of one Martian year (nearly two Earth years). *Surveyor* completed its main mission in 2001, but it continues to send back important data. *Mars Odyssey*

Sunset on Mars, as photographed by the Viking I Lander, which touched down on the red planet on July 20, 1976.

The Mars Global Surveyor, *seen here in an artist's rendition, has helped find evidence of water on the red planet.*

joined *Surveyor* in orbit in October 2001. Previous missions had pointed to the possibility of ice or water on Mars. *Odyssey*'s job was to find it.

In May 2002, *Odyssey* did find strong evidence of water—not just some frost, but enough ice to fill Lake Michigan twice if it melted! The layer of dirty ice lies less than 3 feet (1 m) beneath the surface of Mars's southern pole. In the summer of

2003, scientists, using data from both *Surveyer* and *Odyssey*, found evidence of even more water at Mars's northern pole. But how could a satellite high in orbit know the ice is there? It had help from an instrument called a gamma-ray spectrometer (GRS). The GRS detects and measures energy in the form of gamma rays that hydrogen atoms give off. *Odyssey* team members were on the lookout for signs of hydrogen because it combines with oxygen to make water. In fact, hydrogen is most

Many of the surface features of Mars are visible in this image of Mars.

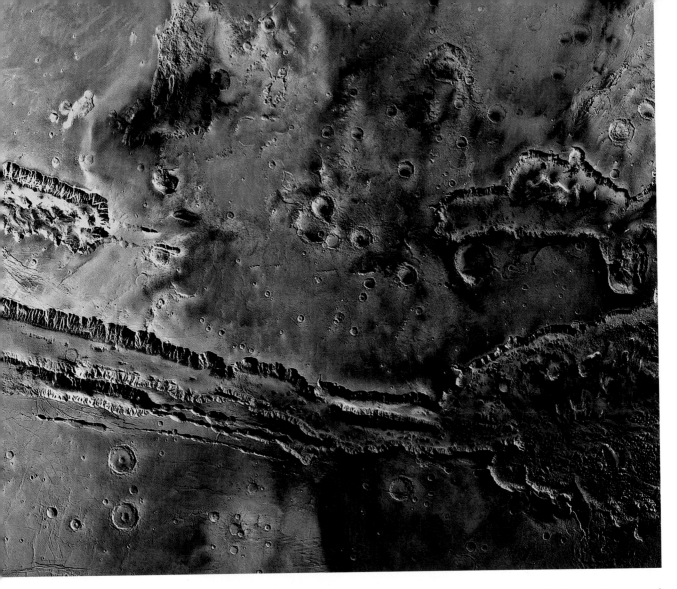

The Viking *probe captured this image of Valle Marineris, a 2,500-mile-long (4,000 km) canyon in Mars's northern hemisphere.*

likely to be found in the form of water or ice. *Odyssey* detected large amounts of hydrogen on Mars.

If there is ice on Mars, might there be life too? Other missions to the red planet hope to find out. The European Space Agency launched *Mars Express* in June 2003. *Express*'s lander, the *Beagle 2*, will be able to perform astrobiology and chemistry experiments. Also launching in the summer of 2003 were two new NASA Mars rovers—*Spirit* and *Opportunity*. Each rover carries everything needed to conduct tests on rocks and soil, process images, and gather other data for about ninety Martian days.

Other missions in the works include the 2005 launch of *Mars Reconnaissance Orbiter*. This is a powerful satellite that will be able to "see" the surface more closely than other orbiting probes. By 2010, NASA hopes to launch a more advanced, long-range rover. It may lead the way to a mission that would be able to return Martian rock and soil samples to Earth. With the help of other nations, Russia proposes to send a human crew to Mars. Russian scientists estimate that it would take 440 days to reach the planet. The six-person crew would then have two months to explore before returning to Earth.

Jupiter and Its Moons

Jupiter, the largest planet in our solar system is not a likely candidate for life. But some of its moons may be. Callisto, Europa, and Ganymede are icy worlds

The Mars Meteorite: Proof of Life?

In December 1984, geologist Roberta Score found a 4 3/4-pound (2 kilogram) potato-shaped meteorite in Antarctica. The space rock arrived on Earth some 16 million years ago, possibly after a comet or asteroid slammed into Mars, sending chunks of rock into space. The meteorite is billions of years old and existed on Mars when the planet may have had liquid water. The rock contains magnetic crystals, some of which are identical to crystals produced by certain bacteria on Earth. Some experts say the crystals are simply the result of mineral processes. Others believe the crystals are the remains of ancient bacteria. After examining the crystals, astrobiologist Kathie Thomas-Keprta and others published a paper in August 2002. They had found that the crystals required a living process to form. The debate goes on.

Once the probe Galileo *completed its six-year journey to Jupiter and its moons in December 1995, it began sending back images like this one, of the icy surface of Jupiter's moon Europa.*

that may hide liquid water beneath their surfaces. And Io is the most volcanically active body in our solar system. The *Pioneer* and *Voyager* spacecraft got the first close-up looks at Jupiter and its moons in the 1970s. The *Galileo* craft zeroed in for an even closer inspection and has been sending information back to Earth about the Jupiter system since 1995.

Of Jupiter's moons, Europa is the most likely to have life. Ice covering Europa's surface may be 3 miles (5 kilometers) thick. With a temperature of -260°F (-162° C), it's possible that the moon's entire ocean could be frozen. But the gravity of Jupiter and the other moons are constantly tugging on Europa. This pulling and stretching might warm the planet beneath the ice and keep at least part of the ocean liquid. NASA is considering sending a spacecraft to orbit Europa. The orbiter would determine whether Europa does have a liquid ocean and, if so, how thick the frozen and melted layers are.

Saturn and Titan

Like Jupiter, Saturn is not a good candidate for life. Its moon Titan, though, is the only other body in the solar system besides Earth to have a thick atmosphere. Titan's nitrogen-rich atmosphere may be much like that of early Earth. And Titan—which is larger than Mercury—may also have ice.

Voyager 1 provided this beautiful image of Saturn and its rings.

Invasion of the Robots

If a Europa orbiter succeeds, the moon's next visitors may be a couple of robots. First, a robot called a cryobot (cryo means "cold") would land on the surface and melt through the thick ice with its warm "nose." Piggybacking on the cryobot would be a hydrobot, (hydro means "water"). This submarine would dive through the opening and explore Europa's undersea world.

This is an artist's depiction of the spacecraft responsible for carrying out NASA's Cassini-Huygens *mission to Saturn.* Cassini *is the orbiter vehicle, while* Huygens *is the probe that is scheduled to land on Titan, Saturn's largest moon, in December 2004.*

The first spacecraft to fly by Saturn and its moons were *Pioneer 11* and *Voyagers 1* and *2*. All three passed by between 1979 and 1981. In 2004, we will get a much closer look when the *Cassini* spacecraft enters Saturn's orbit. *Cassini* is a joint mission of NASA, the European Space Agency, and Italy's space agency. It launched in 1997 and must travel for seven years to reach its destination. Once there, *Cassini* is set to work for four years, collecting and sending back information. One of the most exciting parts of the *Cassini* mission will be the launch of the *Huygens* (HI-genz) probe. The probe will parachute through Titan's atmosphere and collect as much information as possible about the atmosphere and the surface. Titan is thought to have conditions much like those on Earth before it developed an oxygen atmosphere. On Titan, it may actually "rain" organic molecules. Although scientists don't expect to find life on Titan, they believe that studying it may help us understand how life formed on Earth.

Who Was Huygens?

In 1655, Christiaan Huygens became the first person to figure out correctly that the handle-shaped features visible through a telescope on either side of Saturn could be rings. He was also the first to see the moon Titan.

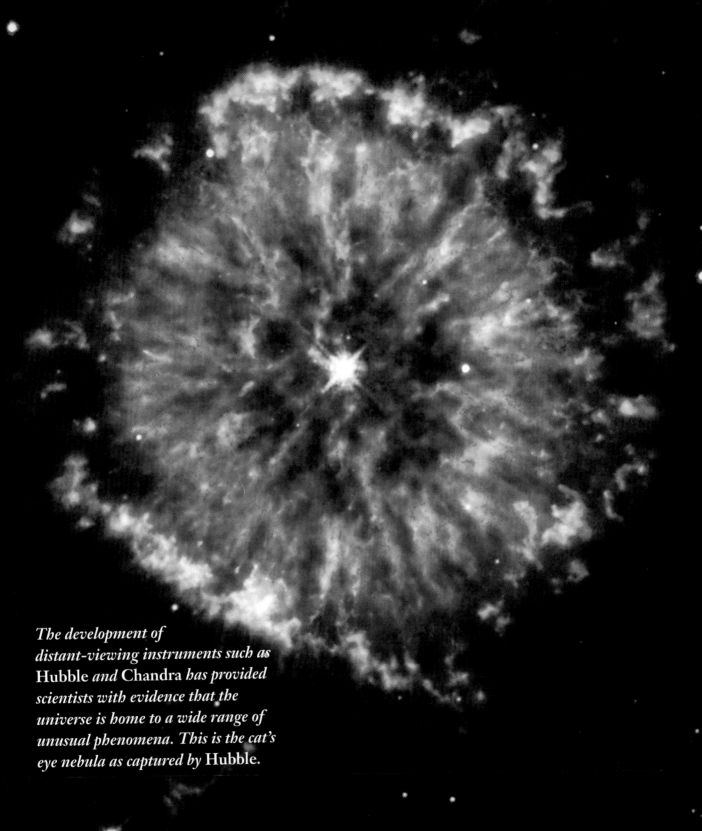

The development of distant-viewing instruments such as **Hubble** *and* Chandra *has provided scientists with evidence that the universe is home to a wide range of unusual phenomena. This is the cat's eye nebula as captured by* **Hubble.**

Chapter Four

Beyond Our Solar System

The search for life is going strong in our own solar system, but what about in other star systems? And how can we investigate across the many **light-years** separating us from them? Some exciting discoveries have already been made. With powerful new technologies, we will be able to search well beyond our solar system.

Planet Finders

Could our solar system, made up of a star and orbiting planets, be unique? This

Star Light, Star Bright

A **light-year** is the distance light travels in one year. One light-year equals 6 trillion miles (9.5 trillion km). Far out, right? It's also way old. Why? The farther away a space object is, the older the picture we see of it. For example, the Andromeda Galaxy is a "neighbor" to our Milky Way Galaxy. It is still 2.2 million light-years away! That means it takes 2.2 million years for its light to reach us. When we look at Andromeda through a telescope, we are seeing how it looked more than 2 million years ago.

seemed unlikely to scientists since the same forces that created our solar system were at work throughout the universe. It seemed much more likely that many stars might anchor their own planetary systems. The difficulty was in finding them. In 1995, scientists finally found the first planet outside our solar system (an **extrasolar** planet). But it wasn't easy.

In recent years, astronomers have discovered planets outside our solar system. This is an image of one of these extrasolar planets.

The Chandra X-ray Observatory captured this image of the spectrum produced by a black hole.

Planets do not emit light of their own. Instead they reflect light from a nearby star. A planet's reflected light gets swallowed up by the bright light from the star, much like the beam of a flashlight disappears when it's shined toward a stadium light at a football field. This means faraway planets are invisible even to the largest telescopes. How can we tell they're there?

Thanks to the force of **gravity**, there's a way to "see" the invisible. As a planet orbits a star, its gravity tugs on the star a bit. For example, as Jupiter, the largest planet in our solar system orbits the Sun, it pulls the Sun around a bit. This shows up as a "wobble" in the Sun's light. Using **spectroscopy**, the study of the light a star gives off, it's possible to detect and measure the wobble. How? When a star moves toward Earth, its light is bluer. When it moves away from Earth, its light is redder. The bigger the shift in color, the larger the orbiting planet is likely to be.

In 1995, spectroscopy enabled Swiss astronomers Didier Queloz and Michel Mayor to discover the first extrasolar planet orbiting a Sun-like star. Since then, astronomers have found more than a hundred extrasolar planets. Most of them are gas giants like Jupiter. Such large planets tug more on their stars and are easier to detect. Debra Fischer, who works with planet hunters Geoffrey Marcy and Paul Butler, believes that with improved equipment, they'll be able to locate much smaller planets. That means that they may find solar systems similar to our own.

Hats Off to *Hubble*

The Hubble image at right, taken in September 2001, shows the effect of a dust storm that obscured the surface of Mars. The image at left was taken three months earlier.

No matter how powerful it is, a ground-based telescope can never get a perfectly clear picture because Earth's atmosphere always blurs the image somewhat. That's why the *Hubble Space Telescope*'s crystal images are so precious. Orbiting 375 miles (600 km) above Earth, *Hubble* zips around the planet at 17,000 miles per hour (27,200 km per hour). That's seventy-seven times faster than a race car! It completes a full orbit every 97 minutes. It can "see" as far as thirteen light-years away. *Hubble* carries cameras and spectrographs and relays its data to Earth by satellite.

June 26, 2001

September 4, 2001

Hubble was launched in 1990. Its mission was to study how the universe began. By observing faraway space objects, *Hubble* has been able to look back in time for clues to the history and evolution of the universe.

Hubble has collected remarkable images and made important discoveries. Some of its accomplishments include finding proof of black holes, showing that quasars are the centers of forming galaxies, witnessing the birth and death of stars, and confirming that the universe is expanding at an increasing speed. It's even been able to detect that Neptune has seasons. *Hubble*'s contribution to science is immense. It is also helping in the search for extraterrestrial life.

Hubble has recorded several developing solar systems. They look like dusty disks around stars. And they seem to be quite common, meaning there may be many solar systems similar to our own. Even more exciting may be *Hubble*'s discovery of a planet outside our solar system with an atmosphere. *Hubble* can't actually "see" the planet, but it detected it—and its sodium atmosphere—when the telescope caught the planet passing in front of its star.

Space shuttle astronauts maintain and upgrade *Hubble* during space walks. Whenever they do, *Hubble*'s equipment gets better. Plans are to keep the super scope going until at least 2010. At that time, it may be moved into a higher orbit or brought back to Earth. If *Hubble*'s work ends in 2010, other space-based telescopes will take its place. Who knows what wonders they might find.

Who Was Hubble?

American astronomer Edwin Hubble (1889–1953) discovered large galaxies outside the Milky Way and determined that such galaxies exist throughout the universe. He was also the first person to find evidence that our universe is expanding.

Extending Our Vision

Now that we know there are other solar systems, how can we get a better look at the extrasolar planets? Several new space missions are designed for planet hunting. Launching first in 2007 is *Kepler*. This space telescope will look for Earth-sized planets around stars some 10,000 light-years from our Sun. When a planet passes between its star and an observer, the star's light dims a bit. *Kepler* will be able to detect the planet and determine its size and orbit.

The *Space Interferometry Mission* (SIM) should launch in 2009. It will be able to find planets around the two hundred stars closest to the Sun. Since these planets are closer to us than those likely to be found by *Kepler*, follow-up missions may be able to learn more about them.

One such mission is *Darwin*, set to launch around 2014. This is not the famous scientist who formed the theory of evolution, but a group of six space telescopes designed to look for signs of life on faraway Earth-like planets. *Darwin* is a mission of the European Space Agency. It will survey a thousand nearby stars for signs of small, rocky planets similar to Earth. Using spectroscopes, *Darwin* will be able to detect whether the planets have atmospheres, and, if so, what they are made of. How does knowing what's in a planet's atmosphere help in finding life? Take Earth as an example. Plants give off oxygen during photosynthesis, and bacteria and other living things produce methane. Finding large enough amounts of either of

Strength in Numbers

An **interferometer** links two or more telescopes to increase their power. On Earth, the Keck Interferometer combines the power of two telescopes atop Hawaii's Mauna Kea.

these elements could point to life on another world. Spectroscopy can also detect water vapor.

NASA's planet-hunting missions include the *Terrestrial Planet Finder (TPF)*. *TPF* will find and study Earth-like planets around as many as 150 stars up to forty-five light-years away. *TPF* will also focus on the dust disks surrounding stars where planets are born. It may help answer questions about planet formation. It is possible that *Darwin* and *TPF* will be combined into one mission. Either way, the planet finders will be on the lookout!

Many scientists now believe that it is possible that some other form of life exists in the universe. But they don't expect it to resemble the "little green men" or "greys" of science fiction.

Chapter Five

Little Green Men?

It's hard to know how long people have dreamed about aliens. Some of the earliest accounts date to the second century A.D., when Lucian of Samosata wrote of frog-eating aliens from the Moon and the Sun. In the nineteenth century, Jules Verne and H. G. Wells wrote books such as *From the Earth to the Moon* and *War of the Worlds*.

Today, the idea of finding other beings like us on the Moon, Sun, or Mars seems silly. But a little more than 100 years ago,

H. G. Wells' famous story War of the Worlds *tells of aliens from Mars that launch a vicious armed invasion of Earth. A 1938 radio broadcast of an adaptation of* War of the Worlds *was taken by many listeners as an actual news report and caused terror and panic on the East Coast.*

at least one important astronomer—and plenty of regular folks—did believe in Martians. Percival Lowell devoted himself to the study of a network of lines on the surface of Mars. Lowell was convinced that the lines were canals that had been built by Martians to channel water from the planet's polar ice caps. He drew sketches of the canals and wrote three books explaining his theories. The trouble was, other astronomers couldn't see the canals, even though some of them used telescopes that were more powerful than Lowell's. Today, we know that Lowell's canals were illusions. But spacecraft have found what resemble dry riverbeds, pointing to a time when the red planet did have water. A search for Martians today focuses on fossilized signs of life and extremophiles. Rather than little green men, it's much more likely that Martians would be little green microbes.

Listening for Clues

Scientists busy with **SETI** (Search for Extraterrestrial Intelligence) don't believe in canal-building Martians. They do believe that there may be intelligent civilizations in the universe, though. It's their mission to find evidence of them. To do that, they listen for signals from such civilizations using instruments right here on Earth. Their "ears" are radio telescopes. These telescopes look like giant satellite dishes, but instead of picking up hundreds of television channels, they pick up space noise in the form of radio waves.

Why radio waves? For one thing, they travel well. Radio

The Drake Equation

SETI pioneer Frank Drake devised an equation in 1961 to determine how many intelligent civilizations might exist in our galaxy. Here it is:

$$N = R \times f_p \times n_e \times f_l \times f_i \times f_c \times L$$

N   is the number of extraterrestrial civilizations.
R   is the number of stars formed in the galaxy each year.
f_p is the fraction of stars with planets.
n_e is the number of planets per star able to support life.
f_l is the fraction of planets where life exists.
f_i is the fraction of planets with intelligent life.
f_c is the fraction of planets with intelligent life that can also communicate across the stars.
L   is the amount of time a civilization capable of such communication exists.

Of the seven factors on the right side of the equation, only one, R, is known. R is about 25. This is the number of stars formed in the galaxy each year. You get this number by dividing the number of stars in the galaxy (about 400 billion) by the galaxy's age (about 15 billion). The other six factors are educated guesses. As we learn more about extrasolar planets and the likelihood of life on them, estimates for the factors will change. Let's plug some educated guesses into the equation and see what happens.

$25 \times 0.5 \times 0.5 \times 1 \times 25 \times 0.1 \times 0.1 \times 500 = 30$ Right now, 30 is our best guess of how many intelligent civilizations might exist in our galaxy.

waves travel at the speed of light and can pass right through dust clouds on their way through space. This means that radio telescopes can "see" farther than light telescopes, because dust clouds often block light. An advanced civilization might use radio waves the way we do—to communicate. So they seem like a good thing to search for.

Astronomer Frank Drake was one of the first to listen for extraterrestrial radio waves. He began his search in 1960. So far, SETI hasn't heard any incoming messages from ET. But there have been some exciting moments. Strange signals intercepted in 1997 turned out to be from a European research satellite. But an unusual signal recorded in 1977 still hasn't been explained. It's known as the "Wow!" signal. The thirty-seven second signal came from the constellation Sagittarius. It was so out of the ordinary, that astronomer Jerry Ehman scribbled "Wow!" next to the printout of the sound. The same signal hasn't been heard again, and it's still a big mystery.

ET or X-Files?

If you've ever seen a Klingon on *Star Trek*, you've seen a typical alien—at least what's typical in people's imaginations. For hundreds of years, people have imagined Martians, Venusians, Moon creatures, and others shaped like humans. Most of the aliens have two legs, two arms, and a head with eyes. They may have blue skin or pointed ears, but they're still pretty much people.

It's doubtful that real aliens would look much like us. After all, when you compare living things on Earth, you find many types and sizes of creatures, each specially adapted to live in its environment. Bacteria make up the largest number of living things on Earth. The ability of bacteria and archaea to live in extreme environments make it likely that life on another planet might also be of the tiny variety. But what of intelligent

Help Search for ET: *SETI@Home*

Using a simple computer screensaver that you can download at *http://setiathome.ssl.berkeley.edu*, your computer can help SETI analyze data collected from the Arecibo Radio Observatory. Who knows, maybe you could be the one to find signals from extraterrestrial life.

or more advanced life? If Frank Drake's equation is correct, there could be a number of civilizations in our galaxy alone that might be able to communicate with us. What might they be like?

Seth Shostak is a SETI astronomer. He wrote *Sharing the Universe*, a book in which he describes what aliens might be like. He believes that aliens able to communicate with us across space are probably animals rather than plants or very small forms such as bacteria or archaea. Animals move around and must learn to do things such as catch or gather food; this helps them develop intelligence. Aliens are likely to be warm-blooded too. The ability to regulate body temperature makes a creature more active and better able to adjust to climate changes.

Shostak thinks intelligent aliens would probably live on land and move about on legs (possibly more than two). Fingers for picking up and holding things would come in "handy." Other important body parts include eyes to take in information about the environment and ears to hear and aid in communication. In fact, says Shostak, all the human senses

Dr. Seth Shostak is a scientist with the SETI (Search for Extraterrestrial Intelligence) project. Among other things, SETI monitors radio waves from outer space for signs of life elsewhere in the universe.

Design an Alien

Use the information in this book and other sources to design an alien. You can put your alien anywhere you choose. Don't worry about whether life might be able to exist on the planet or not. Just have fun figuring out what the alien life-form would be like and how it would be adapted to live in its world. How might an alien that lives on a low-gravity planet get around? What special abilities might an alien living in a very cold or very hot world need? What would it eat? Would it have enemies? Draw pictures of your creation and write about the alien's world and how it fits in.

would be useful to an alien. And because it works well to have the sensory organs up from the ground to get a good look (or sniff) at things, these organs might be located on top of the alien's body. In animals, the sensory organs are also located close to the brain. So Shostak says ET will have a head with a brain inside.

Shostak does not think aliens would look much like us. Even on Earth, humans look very different from other animals. But studying how animals have evolved on Earth is helpful in figuring out what they might be like on another planet. Living things—no matter where they exist—need to find food, raise young, and survive in their environment. So the environment will help shape the life it supports.

Glossary

Archaea—one of the three main types of life. Archaea are microscopic organisms differing from bacteria that include many extremophiles, or extreme-loving microbes.

asteroid—a large space rock

astrobiology—the study of life beyond Earth. Scientists who specialize in astrobiology are astrobiologists.

atmosphere—the blanket of gases that surround a planet or other body in space

Big Bang—the name for the birth of the universe 15 billion years ago

comet—a ball of rock and ice orbiting the Sun. When it gets close enough to the Sun, some of the ice melts, leaving a trail (the comet's tail) behind it.

element—one of more than 100 substances that contain only one kind of atom. Carbon is an element.

extrasolar—orbiting stars other than the Sun

extraterrestrial—existing or coming from beyond Earth; a life-form from beyond Earth

extremophile—a living thing that thrives in environments of extreme heat, cold, pressure, or toxicity

gravity—the force that pulls objects toward eachother

hydrothermal vent—a crack in Earth's crust at the bottom of the ocean which spews out heat and chemicals

interferometer—a combination of two or more telescopes linked together to increase their power

interstellar—existing between stars

light-year—the distance light travels in one year. One light-year equals 6 trillion miles (9.5 trillion km)

meteorite—a piece of rock from space that hits the surface of a moon, planet, or other space body

microbe/microorganism—a microscopic living thing

National Aeronautics and Space Administration (NASA)—the United States' space agency

nebula—a cloud of gases, dust, and other compounds formed by an exploding star

orbit—to travel around a particular object in space; the path an object takes as it travels around another object in space

organic molecules—tiny particles of carbon-based substances

photosynthesis—the process in which plants use the Sun's energy to produce food

SETI—Search for Extraterrestrial Intelligence, an organization dedicated to finding evidence of extraterrestrial intelligence by listening for radio waves

spectroscopy—the study of space objects based on the light and radiation they give off

spectrum—the pattern made by light when it is split into its separate colors

toxic—poisonous

To Find Out More

Books

Dorling Kindersley Publishing Staff. *Space Encyclopedia*. New York: DK Publishing, 2000.

Jefferis, David. *Alien Lifesearch: Quest for Extraterrestrial Organisms*. New York: Crabtree, 1999.

Lippincott, Kristen. *Astronomy*. New York: DK Publishing, 1999.

McDonald, Kim. *Life in Outer Space: The Search for Extraterrestrials*. Austin, TX: Raintree-Steck-Vaughn, 2001.

Spangenburg, Ray, and Kit Moser. *Life on Other Worlds*. Danbury, CT: Scholastic Inc., 2002.

Organizations and Online Sites

Discovery Space Guide

http://dsc.discovery.com/guides/space/space.html

Read features, view Hubble images, explore the space station, and even get a weather report for another planet.

Hubblesite

http://hubblesite.org

Features a collection of news, images, games, and more from the *Hubble Space Telescope*.

NASA Astrobiology Institute

http://nai.arc.nasa.gov/students/index.cfm

Pose your questions to a pro in the "Ask an Astrobiologist" section or play one of three interactive games and activities, including:

Astro-Venture *http://quest.arc.nasa.gov/projects/astrobiology/ astroventure/avhome.html*   Search for and design a habitable planet with help from NASA scientists.

Habitable Worlds *http://nai.arc.nasa.gov/astrotech/solar index.cfm* Search the solar system for signs of life. Pick a planet and learn its vital statistics and whether it could support life.

Mysteries of Microbes *http://quest.arc.nasa.gov/projects/ astrobiology/fieldwork/index.html*   Follow scientists in the field as they study microbes and gather clues about what extraterrestrial life might be like.

NASA Planet Quest
http://planetquest.jpl.nasa.gov
This site contains the latest news on the search for extrasolar planets, including current and upcoming missions and several animated shows, one of which explores the four main ways to search for extrasolar planets.

NOVA: Hunt for Other Worlds
http://www.pbs.org/wgbh/nova/worlds
This site, based on a PBS *NOVA* episode, allows you to search the stars for planets and signs of life.

Who's Out There? Searching for Extraterrestrial Intelligence
http://www.seti.org/game
This interactive game allows you to decide where and how to search for signs of extraterrestrial intelligence.

A Note on Sources

Scientists are learning more about space and the possibility of finding extraterrestrial life every day. It's important to keep up with the latest. That's why the Internet, especially the Web sites of NASA, SETI, and the Hubble Space Telescope, were so useful in writing this book. Recently published books and magazines such as *Science*, *Scientific American*, and *Discover* are also great sources. But the best resources of all are the scientists who are doing the work.

Read the newspaper. Surf the Web. That's how you can keep up with scientists' search for alien life. Several of the missions mentioned in this book will unfold after it's been printed. So, it's up to you to stay tuned.

—*Rhonda Lucas Donald*

Index

Numbers in *italics* indicate illustrations.

About the Author

Rhonda Lucas Donald has been writing books for children and teachers for eighteen years. She has published several books about protecting animals and the environment and numerous articles in magazines such as *Ranger Rick* and the newspaper *EarthSavers*. Rhonda specializes in writing about science, and she particularly likes to write about animals and space. She has been interested in the search for extraterrestrial life since watching *Star Trek* as a kid. She is doing her part to help find proof of intelligent life by analyzing radio telescope signals for SETI on her computer. Rhonda lives in Rocky Mount, North Carolina, with her husband Bruce, dog Maggie, and cats Sophie and Tory.